Tap Tap Tap

Written by Natasha Paul

Collins

tap

pat

3

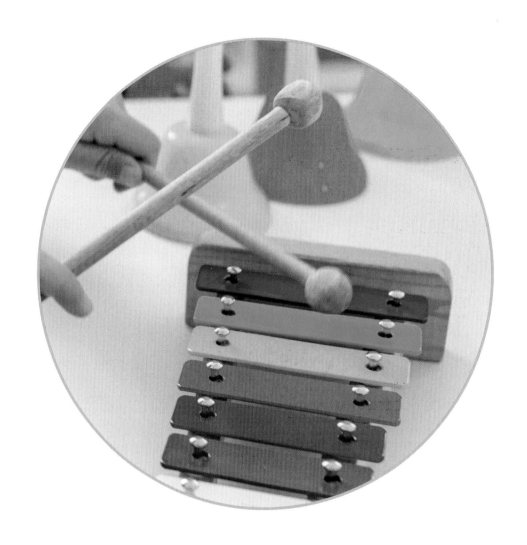

tap

pat

pat

pat
. . .

pat

pat

tap

sit

tap

sit

14

 Review: After reading

Use your assessment from hearing the children read to choose any GPCs and words that need additional practice.

Read 1: Decoding

- Use grapheme cards to make any words you need to practise. Model reading those words, using teacher-led blending.
- Look at the "I spy sounds" pages (14–15) together. Ask the children to point out as many things as they can in the picture that begin with the /p/ sound. (*pat, panpipes, piano, pencil, panda, purple, painting, peg, peacock, pineapple, planet, pinecone, pumpkin, puppet, penguin, pears, pens*)
- Ask the children to follow as you read the whole book, demonstrating fluency and prosody.

Read 2: Vocabulary

- Look back through the book and discuss the pictures. Encourage the children to talk about details that stand out for them. Use a dialogic talk model to expand on their ideas and recast them in full sentences as naturally as possible.
- Work together to expand vocabulary by naming objects in the pictures that children do not know.
- On pages 2 and 3, ask the children to mime tapping and patting, to check their understanding of the verbs.

Read 3: Comprehension

- Talk about any musical instruments the children have played or heard. Can they mime playing their favourite instrument?
- Turn to page 10. Ask: What are the children using to **tap**? (*sticks*)
- On page 11, ask: Who sits? (e.g. *the girls*) Ask the children to point to a child who is tapping or patting.